What Others are S

LINKED©for Couples Quick Guide to Personalities

"You can't fix him or her, but you can learn to live with them, and *LINKED® for Couples* helps you discover how. I love this quick guide, which is full of real-life examples of how husbands and wives interact with each other when their personalities are different. The authors' wisdom, experience, and knowledge of working with couples and their marriages shines through each page of this excellent marriage book."

**Joyce Zook, Author,
Speaker, Marriage Coach, Certified
Personalities Trainer, and Consultant**

"My marriage ONLY survived because we were both committed to success. Some of our years would have been happier had we had this book. Trial and error was our feeble attempt to achieving a successful marriage. Being a Mobilizer, and my husband a Stabilizer created a challenge. If we had had this book, our marriage would have had less pain and we would have received desired results more efficiently and quickly."

**Sheila Sistare, Retired teacher
and Mobilizer, Married 47 years**

"Good communication is vitally important in all human relationships, especially in marriage. In *LINKED* for Couples, Gilden and Goldfarb, better known as "The Two Lindas," rightly make the point that understanding your spouse's basic personality, what makes them tick, how they tend to handle stress, how they express frustration, affection, and joy, is an essential ingredient in developing good communication between marital partners. This book is chock full of helpful, practical advice for married couples who realize a healthy marriage is always a work in progress."

Baxter Wynn D.Min

"*LINKED® for Couples* is a practical resource for anyone who longs to strengthen their marriage. After clear guidance to help you identify your personality and your spouse's, the Two Lindas show you how those personalities impact the way you relate to one another. This quick guide will equip you to more effectively communicate with your spouse. LINKED® is well worth your time!"

Kathy Howard, Bible teacher and author
of *Unshakeable Faith* and *Lavish Grace*

"With so much divorce, *LINKED˚ for Couples* is a tool that shows how to have a good, loving marriage, where we learn to accept and value one another. It's filled with treasures of ideas to strengthen your marriage and deepen your appreciation of one another. When a marriage is bonded together as one, no matter what happens in life, you can face it together and be a support to one another. I highly recommend this book to all couples and those in premarital counseling."

Carolyn Searls, Author
and Public Speaker

"Whether couples are different or alike, understanding each other is key. This book is a must read for marrieds or couples who are serious about getting married. The quiz alone is worth the price of admission but having a list of words for our tendencies and giving us a Heart Language is gold! Communication is key, and the authors get to the heart of a marriage. I will be gifting this book to my adult daughter who is in a serious relationship. Every counselor or coach should have this book handy in their resource library."

Phylis Mantelli, author, speaker, coach,
podcast co-host *24 Carat Conversations*

"The *LINKED* for Couples Quick Guide to Personalities* is an essential resource for all couples, that offers not only quick tips to help you connect better with your spouse, but also tried and true strategies. You will find your marriage strengthened and you will notice your ability to communicate with others will also improve. It's exciting to discover the positive and negative tendencies for each personality and realize you *can* make positive, healthy changes."

Sheryl Giesbrecht Turner, ThD, author of *It'll Be Okay: Finding God When Doubt Hides the Truth*, www.fromashestobeauty.com

"*LINKED* for Couples* is a book I will use with and recommend to the women and couples I coach to help them understand their and their partner's God-given strengths and needs. So much misunderstanding can be avoided by recognizing our different motivations and desires. I highly recommend *LINKED* for Couples* for engaged and married couples as well as for the professionals who support them."

Debbie W. Wilson, Bible teacher, life coach, and author of *Little Faith, Big God*

"Like vitamins, the LINKED* Quick Guides to Personalities are small, power-packed how-tos. The Two Lindas have expertly outlined *LINKED* for Couples* to communicate in life-giving ways to quickly improve your relationship with your spouse."

PeggySue Wells, bestselling author of 29 books including *The Ten Best Decisions A Single Mom Can Make*

"LINKED© for Couples is like having a personal couple's retreat, complete with aha moments, fun, and improved communication skills. The authors made it simple for me to identify and understand our personalities. I'm a Mobilizer married to an Organizer. This Grin Gal promises you'll add more grins to your relationship as you read this book and incorporate it into your marriage."

Kathy Carlton Willis, God's Grin Gal, speaker and author of *The Grin Gal's Guide to Joy, 7 Trials Every Woman Faces* and others www.kathycarltonwillis.com

"Understanding your mate has never been easier. Reading *LINKED© for Couple*s gives you the basic knowledge you need to not only survive in your marriage but also to thrive. Personality knowledge plus a book full of creative ideas is a winning combination!"

Rhonda Robinson, marketing coach, speaker, award winning author, *FreeFall: Holding Onto Faith When the Unthinkable Strikes*

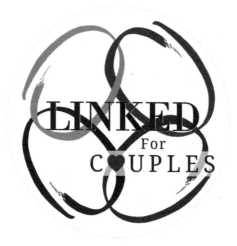

LINKED
For
C♥UPLES

QUICK GUIDE
TO
PERSONALITIES

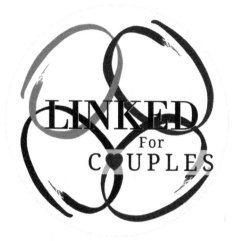

QUICK GUIDE
TO
PERSONALITIES

Maximizing Heart Connections
One Link at a Time

Linda Gilden and Linda Goldfarb

Bold Vision Books
PO Box 2011
Friendswood, Texas 77549

Copyright © Linda Gilden and Linda Goldfarb 2021
ISBN 9781946708-58-8
Library of Congress Control Number Available
LINKED® is a registered trademark symbol

Published by Bold Vision Books, PO Box 2011,
Friendswood, Texas 77549
www.boldvisionbooks.com

Logo and Cover Design by Linda Goldfarb
Emojis Design by Jonathan Bishop
Interior by kae Creative Solutions

Published in the United States of America.

Dedication

Without the love, support, and dedication of
our husbands, John and Sam,
we (the Two Lindas) would not be equipped
to write this book.

We dedicate the words and stories within to
married couples everywhere.
May you find new ways to love the one who is
your mate for life.

Table of Contents

Foreword

There are a few essential truths and tools every couple needs in their marriage toolbox to create a long-lasting love. *LINKED® for Couples* is one of those.

My husband, Bill, and I are most known for our bestseller, *Men Are Like Waffles, Women Are Like Spaghetti.* Our ministry is *Love-Wise,* and we say that we park ourselves on the corner of *God's Love* and *God's Wisdom.* We are kindred hearts with Linda Gilden and Linda Goldfarb because they too desire to equip, encourage, and enrich couples with practical, biblical, and applicable tools. We all value helping couples multiply appreciation of their mates and treasure how God designed them.

Bill and I share with audiences that men *compartmentalize* their thinking. Visualize the top of a waffle: boxes separated by walls. A guy places one issue in each box. They go into a box, identify the problem, assign a solution, then move on. And if they see the problem but don't know a solution— they move on!

Conversely, the word picture that captures the way women think is a plate of spaghetti. Women's minds *integrate* meaning one issue connects to every other issue. If you follow one noodle around a plate of spaghetti, it seems to touch every other noodle on the plate. Women travel through their lives connecting to the people and things that matter most to them.

People follow up our talks with the question: "I am a female, and I am more "waffle-like, why?" Or "I am a male and have some spaghetti characteristics, so what's up with that?"

We reply *Men are like Waffles, Women are like Spaghetti* is the biblical and biological base, but there are many reasons people do what they do. Our God-designed personalities and motivations are a big part of our complex interactions. This is where *LINKED® for Couples* enters as a vital tool to help individuals learn how to better understand and appreciate these unique motivational traits. The two Lindas take the complex and make relating to one another easier to comprehend, process, and apply.

LINKED® for Couples is power packed with lots of great methods, ideas, and activities to help us live inspired to love. This book in your hands stirs us all to see our mates from a *by design* viewpoint. These truths have proven to be a bonding agent for me and my husband, and these principles can be super-glue for you too.

Are you getting excited to turn the page and begin the fascinating journey of discovering the best about your mate and yourself?

I am enthused for you. I know this book will build and bless your marriage! The two Lindas are trusted voices who bring truth to their readers. By reading and living out *LINKED® for Couples* you will fall in love with your mate all over again. You will also gain essential skills to protect your marriage. 2 Timothy 1:14 admonishes us to "Guard the treasure entrusted to you" and *LINKED® for Couples* will help you do that.

Are you ready for some wonderful reading with pleasant results of a harmonious love and life? Set aside time to read and process this practical manuscript then anticipate the good, the beautiful, and the best God will do for you!

Pam Farrel
Author of 52 books
Co-Director of Love-Wise
www.Love-wise.com

Chapter 1
Get Started

Graham and Sarah fell in love in high school. Most of their dates were spent doing their favorite fun activities including dancing, going to concerts, ballgames, and browsing museums. Graham was the participant, and Sarah was the spectator. She never minded when Graham took the dance floor with a friend. Because these activities required minimal conversation and Graham and Sarah's roles were different, they didn't talk a lot.

After Graham and Sarah married, Sarah came to Graham with a serious conversation. "Something is missing from our relationship. I'm not sure what it is. But a part of me feels disconnected from you."

> We are different by design and discovering those differences can help us to overcome difficulties before they grow into fractured relationships.

"I love being with you," Graham assured her. "We have so much fun together."

"I know," she said. "But I feel like we are just *being*. We don't really talk. Then when we have to make a major decision, neither of us knows what to say."

Graham and Sarah had just discovered an essential aspect of a good marriage—communication between husband and wife. And how we communicate is rooted in our personality. Husband-to-wife relationships often fail to grow deeper because spouses don't understand one another.

What about you?

Do you love your spouse, but feel like you don't understand each other?

Do you long to have a deeper connection with your life's partner?

Is your marriage thriving or merely surviving?

Is there conflict in your home that you would like to convert to peace?

When your marriage is struggling to thrive, be assured you're not alone. While today we, Linda Gilden (Rose) and Linda Goldfarb (Goldie), are thriving with our husbands, both of us have experienced difficulties in our marriages. Here are snippets from our journeys.

After our honeymoon, we (Rose and John) drove from South Carolina to our new home in New Jersey. It was a long drive but we took turns driving and made it safely.

We walked in the door of our new apartment (about the size of a current tiny house) and unloaded the car full of wedding presents. We were upstairs in our little bedroom making up the bed with our new sheets and wedding gift bedspread when the phone rang. John went to answer it and when he came back he said, "I've got to go."

"Got to go? Where? When will you be back? Can I go with you?" I asked.

"All that is classified. I can't answer any of those questions."

"What? I don't think I signed up for this. I thought we were going to share everything, communicate with each other, and support each other no matter what. How can I support you if I don't even know where you are?"

"You know I have been serving on this detail for over a year. And you knew it was classified."

"Yes, but I didn't know that included me. I'm your wife."

Yes, you are and I am so proud of that. But I still can't tell you where I'm going or for how long."

"But I don't think classified includes the wife. I married you for better or worse. You are getting ready to take our only car and I don't know anybody here in the apartment building. I am going to have to sleep in a strange place all by myself?" My voice rose.

"I'm sorry. But in the military, some things are just secret. I shouldn't be gone more than a few days."

Growing a heart-connected relationship must include intentional communication.

I know now that I could have saved myself a lot of pouting and tears if I had knowledge of the personalities at that time.

My new husband introduced me to the Mobilizer personality on our first night in New Jersey.

They said he had to go – he went – wife or no wife.

They said not to tell anyone what he was doing –he kept his mouth shut–wife or no wife

The problem was that I was not a Mobilizer. I had no clue what that was or meant. I was an Organizer and knew exactly how I thought our first night should go. And here the first night, I saw a side of my husband that I was unfamiliar with. I knew marriage was going to be a time of discovery for both of us but it would have been so much easier to get to know one another if we had known the personalities.

My (Goldie) marriage journey, like my personality, falls on the other side of the spectrum from Rose's. Sam and I had experienced divorce and entered our marriage with a lot of unhappy relational history behind us. I brought my seven-year-old son and three-year-old daughter into our relationship while Sam's family consisted of Big John, a chestnut colored Tennessee Walking Horse, and a yard full of German Shorthaired Pointers. As a blended family, we enjoyed time together hunting and fishing, but quickly navigated to the negative corners of our relationship, where a lot of she said, he said ensued with vigor.

"You're not their biological father, so you can't possibly understand!" I said this too many times. And I never took into consideration the wisdom Sam was providing, because I was too caught up in the emotional aspects of the situation.

Sam's tendency to want things done correctly overflowed on the children. "I don't care if she's only four, how you hold your fork says a lot about your upbringing!" That prompted a defensive posture on my side.

My impatience to get tasks completed quickly became the catalyst of demeaning my husband. "Sam, since when does taking a nap last four hours? Get up! We have a lot to get done." Yikes, can you say, "Hello Ms. Bossy Pants!"

"Linda, can you sit down for a minute and let me show you what I've planned out. If we prepack the truck tonight, get up at 5:30 AM, hit the road at 6:15 AM we can make it to the hunting lease by 7:30 AM. The kids don't even have to change out of their pajamas, they can sleep on the way. Easy peasy." Wow! To say we viewed the world-of-communication through different lenses is an understatement. Thank goodness we discovered the power of connecting our hearts through the personalities. Today, we talk more, care more, and listen more—a great way to grow together.

Both of us (Rose and Goldie) agree, marriage consists of two individuals coming together to love and cherish for a lifetime. We are each different by design, and the challenge for healthy relationships is to blend while remaining uniquely ourselves. Our positive and negative tendencies form our personalities. Understanding ourselves and our spouses happens when we know how personality affects every decision, action, and reaction.

The LINKED four basic personality types are:

Mobilizer

Get-it-done spouse

Socializer

Life-of-the-party spouse

Stabilizer

Keep-it-peaceful spouse

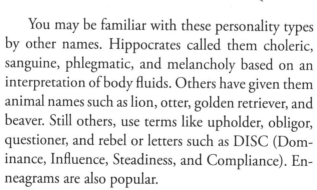

Organizer

Everything-in-order spouse

You may be familiar with these personality types by other names. Hippocrates called them choleric, sanguine, phlegmatic, and melancholy based on an interpretation of body fluids. Others have given them animal names such as lion, otter, golden retriever, and beaver. Still others, use terms like upholder, obligor, questioner, and rebel or letters such as DISC (Dominance, Influence, Steadiness, and Compliance). Enneagrams are also popular.

In every method of assessment, there is a powerful personality, a playful personality, a peaceful personality, and a purposeful personality. No matter what you call them, each of the four corresponds with one of these descriptions. Discovering how your personality interacts with the personality of your spouse helps overcome difficulties before they crumble into fractured relationships.

Understanding how personalities interact is life-changing for couples who

- want to make their relationship stronger
- want to understand each other
- are busy, yet value one another
- desire to see their families thrive
- long to connect at a deeper level to feel closer and more like-minded

Understanding how your two personalities blend is key. To really get to know each other goes beyond just where you're from, where you went to school, and how many siblings you have. To thrive, be willing to grab a communication shovel and dig deep into your relationship, your heart, how you think, and how you react to big and small situations.

Chapter 2
Who Are You?

John and I (Rose) stood in the hall waiting for the elevator to arrive. Even though we were only four floors up, I dreaded the short elevator ride with a car full of strangers. John on the other hand smiled and made small talk with others who were also waiting.

I am an Organizer. I like the people I hang around with but to get in the elevator and ride four floors with complete strangers just wasn't my cup of tea. I would prefer to wait until an empty elevator arrived and then get on so I didn't have to talk to anyone. John, on the other hand, couldn't wait to see who he was going to meet on the short ride down.

Sure enough, the elevator arrived and the doors opened. There stood another couple. John grabbed my hand and took a step forward. I realized my choices were to follow him and try to be congenial or to let go of his hand and wait until the next car, leaving him with the awkward decision of whether to get on without me or step back and wait with me.

I chose to follow and push myself into the farthest corner from the other folks. John stood in the middle. Before the door even shut, John said, "Hello, how y'all doing this morning?"

The other man whose name we later found out was Kyle, replied, "We are great. Where you folks from?"

Oh no. Two Socializer personalities on the same elevator. I backed even farther into the corner. My back was against the wall and I halfway smiled. "We're from South Carolina," John said. "How 'bout y'all?"

"Michigan."

This conversation continued until we felt the familiar bump of the elevator coming to a stop on the first floor. I had feared the elevator might take so long that these two would make dinner plans for the four of us. Thankful when the door opened and once we exited would never have to see Kyle and Peggy again, I grabbed John's hand and pulled him through the door.

Your personality is most likely different from your spouse. No worries, you were designed differently for a reason.

You might ask the question – How long does it take a Socializer to make a new best friend? The answer – No more than four floors in an elevator.

My Organizer personality finds those situations terribly uncomfortable, but I am learning to let my halfway smile be a little broader and maybe even let myself timidly say, "Good-bye" as we leave the elevator.

Now it's time for you to discover your personality by taking the assessment test below. Go with your first thought, be as honest as you can, and don't over think your answers. For best results, don't consider which is the better or best choice. Mark one answer per question.

1 - You've been assigned a project to complete in two weeks. You
    a - get it done right away, even if you have to stay up late
    b - procrastinate but finish well at the last minute
    c - have a challenge finishing as you want the project perfect
    d - take your time, finishing at an easy pace

2 - Friends would describe you as
    a - bold and to the point
    b - fun and entertaining
    c - witty and detail-oriented
    d - likable and easy-going

3 - You find yourself in a public conversation. You
    a - laugh sometimes and enjoy joining in
    b - listen and contribute only when needed
    c - might interrupt with a solution for most problems
    d - listen and offer encouragement

4 - The most important thing to have in life is
   a - peace
   b - perfection
   c - fun
   d - control

5 - When it comes to friends, you
   a - make a lot of friends easily
   b - have little need for friends
   c - make friends cautiously
   d - get along with everyone

6 - When choosing a place to eat, you
   a - act spontaneously
   b - take a while to decide
   c - have particular places in mind
   d - don't have a preference

7 - Your ideal weekend would include
   a - traveling to a new place
   b - having quality time with your spouse
   c - learning a new skill
   d - having a pajama day

8 - When you are stressed, you
   a - find a quiet place to rest
   b - call a friend and go shopping
   c - get away to a spot where you're alone and
       can recharge
   d - work out

9 - If you look in your closet, you will see
   a - all the hangers turned the same way and
       clothes neatly hung

b - bright colors and fun patterns

c - trendy outfits with all pieces hanging together

d - a lot of comfortable clothes

10 - When your mate is hurting, you

    a - cry with your loved one

    b - wrap your arms around your spouse in a big hug

    c - tell your mate to be strong and get back into life

    d - try to make him or her feel better by planning something fun

11 - When you are in a crowd, you

    a - enjoy all your new best friends

    b - wish you could hurry, get home, and put up your feet

    c - retreat to the perimeter to talk to someone you already know

    d - work the crowd to identify contacts

12 - People often say you are

    a - controlling

    b - fun-loving

    c - encouraging

    d - laid back

13 - Driving one morning, you see a man knock over a lady and flee. You most likely

    a - call 9-1-1 and jump to the lady's aid

    b - park, call 9-1-1, and wait

c - pass by, hoping she's okay

d - ask if she is alright and text friends to tell what you saw

14 - Getting on an elevator to go four floors, you

a - waste no time starting a conversation with those already inside

b - move to the back corner and hope the elevator is fast

c - smile and stand quietly

d - push the button for your floor and ask the others which floor they'd like

15 - When unexpected company knocks at your door, you

a - turn around and shout "Party!"

b - invite them in and immediately begin tidying up

c - tell them it's good to see them, but you have a headache

d - invite them in, control the short visit, then stand and bid them good-bye

16 - While lying in the hammock by the lake, you

a - nap easily

b - make a checklist for errands

c - invite a friend to join you

d - have a hard time just lying there

17 - Your parents are coming for a visit this week-end. You

a - rush around making sure everything is in place and clean

b - brief the family on how to act and what to do

c - decide the house is clean enough

d - call all the relatives letting them know about the visit

18 - When given the choice, you prefer
  a - to lead
  b - to serve
  c - to research
  d - to entertain

19 - When you are sad, you
  a - read a book
  b - tell a friend
  c - work on a project
  d - take a nap

20 - At meetings when given the opportunity to voice your opinion you
  a - speak up
  b - give your opinion and more
  c - choose your words carefully
  d - say few words

21 - If you were a piece of a puzzle, you would be
  a - the corners
  b - the bright flowers
  c - the straight edges
  d - the background

22 - In life, you tend to be
  a - playful
  b - purposeful
  c - powerful
  d - peaceful

23 - Your car of choice would be
    a - economical and safe
    b - comfortable and easy to maintain
    c - sporty and fun
    d - stylish and dependable

24 - You are drawn to
    a - things done the right way
    b - things done the fast way
    c - things done the easy way
    d - things done the fun way

25 - People who know you would say you are
    a - competitive
    b - cautious
    c - committed
    d - carefree

26 - Your peers describe you as
    a - results-oriented
    b - service-oriented
    c - detail-oriented
    d - pleasure-oriented

Circle your answers on the assessment key in the back of the book and record the sum of your tallies in each column. Transfer those numbers on the personality-designated line below.

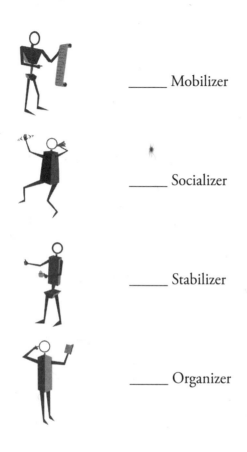

_____ Mobilizer

_____ Socializer

_____ Stabilizer

_____ Organizer

The highest number is your dominant personality. The next highest number is your secondary personality. Write third highest score on the third line, this is a complementary personality.

Dominant   _____

Secondary   _____

Complementary   _____

Your personality is most likely different from your spouse. No worries, you were designed differently for a reason. If your personalities are similar, woohoo, your common links will prove to be a powerful combination.

We link our personalities in a clockwise pattern, Socializer, Stabilizer, Organizer, Mobilizer according to the brain science supporting the connections between personalities. In some cases, you may wind up with three top personalities, dominant, secondary, and complimentary. We call these the *likely blends of your personality smile.* Write in your top personality types on the Smile diagram below. Notice how these combinations naturally link together.

Stabilizer-**Socializer**-Mobilizer
Organizer-**Stabilizer**-Socializer
Mobilizer-**Organizer**-Stabilizer
Socializer-**Mobilizer**-Organizer

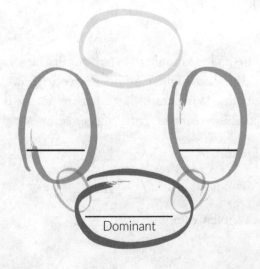

Dominant

Some of us are no-assessment-needed, hands-down one distinct personality, while others exhibit characteristics of more than one type. But for the most part, you and your mate will have a dominant personality.

In some cases, *unlikely blends* occur such as the ones below.

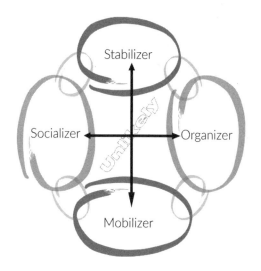

These combinations usually occur based on learned behavior resulting from interacting with others in a personality that isn't our natural characteristic. This unlikely combination can happen when we've learned that behaving a certain way accomplishes a desired goal. Check out our free Blended Personalities downloadable link in the appendix.

In the next few sections we look at each personality to help you connect deeper to your link and the links of those you love.

Chapter **3**
Behavior Identifiers

Each personality has characteristics unique to that type, and each type holds common characteristics. Here are behavior identifiers for the four personalities. Recognizing these traits in those you love will help you communicate in ways that enable you and your spouse to feel heard and understood.

You might be a MOBILIZER if ...

- You complete tasks quickly around the house.

- You like to fix a problem or meet a challenge head on.

- You tend to be focused, direct, and to the point.

- You desire loyalty and appreciation.

- You're frustrated when your home life is out of control.

- You like doing several projects simultaneously.

- You relax by working out.

- You dislike and prefer to avoid high drama and mushy emotions.

Mobilizers are the movers and shakers of the world. They set their goals and move full speed ahead to completion. Mobilizer spouses, though they love their mates, can come across as pushy and having high expectations, especially to their Stabilizer or Socializer mates.

As a Mobilizer, I've learned that because she's a Stabilizer, June is hurt by harsh tones and immediate expectations for change.

"Learning I was a Mobilizer changed my life," says Scott. "My wife called me bossy, but I didn't understand why. I never saw myself that way. I know how things ought to be done and just want the best for both of us. Why couldn't she see that? I've learned that because she's a Stabilizer, June is hurt by harsh tones and immediate expectations for change. Being a Mobilizer has its challenges, but I'm a better husband today because I invite interaction with my wife. Our relationship improved when I learned not to dictate my wants to her."

Quick Tip: If you are a Mobilizer, give your spouse plenty of time to accomplish tasks. Instead of criticizing a lack of speed, ask how you can help, but don't nag. Then step back and let your spouse accomplish the task their way. Be content with the results and smile.

You might be a SOCIALIZER if...

- You incorporate fun in your daily life.

- You're creative and a natural storyteller.

- You tend to speak a lot, sometimes too much.

- You enjoy attention and approval.

- You're frustrated when life is no longer fun.

- You like easy schedules and to be showered with affection.

- Eating out and/or shopping relaxes you.

- You easily show your emotions.

Socializers enjoy a party. They seek or create fun in everything they do. Even tedious and boring tasks are pleasant when you do them with a Socializer. Socializers feel lonely when they are not surrounded by action. Taking time to relax and be still is difficult and often requires great discipline for the Socializer personality. Those quiet moments are easier for a Socializer when there is a fun activity already scheduled onto the calendar as something to look forward to.

"I'm often called the 'life of the party,'" says Kelly. "I like to have a good time and staying out late with friends makes me happy. What a surprise to realize my love for fun caused my husband a lot of stress. When we went out with others, he usually stood off by himself. When I tried to bring him into a conversation, he wouldn't say much. Later, I'd accuse him of being antisocial and we'd go to bed upset. Since learning I'm a Socializer and he's an Organizer, I realized that socializing charged my emotional batteries but drained his. Exhausted after a day at work, he wanted to rest. We've learned to compromise. I still have fun with friends and family, but I choose to settle down earlier in the evening. It's the best of both worlds since Justin and I are enjoying spending more time with each other."

Quick Tip: There's a time and place for fun. Structured fun with healthy time limits benefits both the Socializer and the less social spouse. Let your gift be a stronger balance of peace and quiet, and your spouse will be more apt to explore your fun options.

You might be a STABILIZER if...

- You gravitate to the easy way of living life.

- You think a bit longer than others before you speak.

- You appreciate respect from your mate, though you won't ask for it.

- You're supportive, easy-going, and handle pressure well.

- You like peace and quiet.

- You're frustrated when your home becomes chaotic.

- Time alone such as watching TV or reading a book relaxes you.

- You bury emotions especially when your feelings are hurt.

Stabilizers enjoy people, in small doses, and shy away from conflict and change.

Recognized as the quiet and relaxed personality, the Stabilizer often has the calmest attitude, yet a lack of vocal excitement can seem boring to a Socializer or weak to a Mobilizer.

Before understanding the personalities, every day was a struggle and there was no looking forward to relaxing weekends.

"I dreaded coming home from the office to a long list of projects waiting on the kitchen counter," Trevor said. "My wife, Mary, is always busy. She likes to garden and go hiking. Diving into another home improvement project is her idea of having fun. It's not mine. Adding a screened back porch with a swing nearly put me six feet under. I don't like confrontation or added work, yet I knew I'd enjoy the two-seater swing. I'm a Stabilizer and she's a Mobilizer. Before understanding the personalities, every day was a struggle and there was no looking forward to relaxing weekends.

"I shared my need for downtime after a long day at the office and Mary was open to me spending 30 minutes to unwind before we discussed her list. Yes, she still makes lists, but I'm not fretting about them anymore. I look the list over and agree on two things I can accomplish in her timeline; she usually gives me a kiss and I hold on for a hug. Today, our marriage is blossoming into win-win weekends with peaceful weekdays."

Quick Tip: As a Stabilizer, your calm and steady temperament is valuable to those around you. Consider sharing your thoughts and opinions more often. And on occasion change up your vocal tempo and tone to engage more frequently with others.

You might be an ORGANIZER if...

- You prefer life done the right way.

- You're loyal and sensitive to loved ones and causes.

- You listen more, speak less, and think a lot.

- You're thoughtful and deliberate.

- You're frustrated when life is imperfect.

- You like quality over quantity.

- Long stretches of silence and plenty of space is relaxing.

Organizers are rule followers who are frequently labeled as perfectionists. They want the right way, every day, which makes life a challenge for them personally and for the ones they love. Because of this perfectionism, Organizers may struggle to accept their spouses' actions unconditionally.

"What a self-revelation to discover my personality drives the way I think as a wife and how I manage my home," Sabrina says. "My attention to detail with my business and my home is by design. My Organizer personality tends to overdo and this is tiring for me and my spouse.

"When my Socializer husband has a choice to sort the laundry or walk the dog, he's out the door before the leash is snapped correctly. 'Close the door and be careful about other dogs on the street,' I call, only to find the door still ajar. Through the window, I see my husband and dog, tumbling on the grass like two kids. That's when my frustration kicks in. What a relief to discover my perfectionist tendency was not an inborn desire to drive myself and everyone around me crazy. Knowing our personality differences allowed me freedom to be who I'm born to be and accept my husband as he was created to be as well. As I focused on William's strengths, I began to enjoy his quirkiness without judgment, exchanging perfectionism for appreciation."

Quick Tip: Accept excellence in lieu of perfectionism to be the best you can and remove pressure from your daily expectations. Don't lower your standards, yet be willing to compromise. Relax, accept that your spouse doesn't do everything according to your expectations and look for opportunities to appreciate your mate.

Chapter 4
Personality Tendencies

Sam and I (Goldie) are completely opposite personality blends. Interesting fact, Sam is the same blend as Rose, Organizer/Stabilizer, and I'm the same as Rose's husband John, Mobilizer/Socializer. So, in essence, Rose and I are writing alongside the personalities we're married to. Which makes what we do so much fun and therapeutic!

For more than six years, Sam and I taught and coached as a couple in our parenting ministries, Parenting Awesome Kids and Parenting Junior Golfers. Since I had studied and taught the personalities a lot longer than him, in the beginning, Sam wasn't as comfortable talking about our personalities and had a hesitancy when it came to fully "buying in" to the value of understanding ourselves and those around us from a behavioral point of view. That is until one mom in our class, Janie, (and many more since then) talked about the transformation she experienced with her children and between her and her husband because of our personality teachings.

"I went home last week determined to implement two things I had learned about the personalities into my daily routine with my girls and my husband. My four-year-old Socializer daughter ran me ragged with all of her drama trauma, while her older Organizer sister stressed me out with her need to do everything perfectly. So, I focused on their emotional needs instead of harping on their actions and wow, the change was almost immediate. My Socializer calmed down and my Organizer became content with doing her best. I also fed into the heart language of my Stabilizer husband, because I learned it was difficult for him to express his emotions. I will tell you all, this personality stuff works!"

From that point forward, Sam not only shares about the personalities with others, he and I are closer because of it.

"One thing I've learned," said Sam. "Understanding my personality doesn't label me, it gives me freedom to be who I was designed to be, and I'm good with that."

The Socializer tends to see the glass half full because she slants toward fun and everyone being happy.

We're (Goldie and Rose) hoping you will be good with it too as you get to know the four personality types and recognize characteristics specific to each one. We note them as positive and negative tendencies. As you look over the charts for the Mobilizer and Socializer, notice some tendencies overlap onto a linking personality. For example, the Mobilizer is not easily discouraged, and the Socializer is optimistic. These are similar traits, yet different. The Socializer tends to see the positive side of situations encouraging everyone to have fun and be happy, while the Mobilizer is more cut-n-dry, and seldom allows anything or anyone to stop him when he's on a mission to get it done.

The Mobilizer and Socializer are extroverts and fast responding, but for different reasons. The Mobilizer gains control by his or her extrovert trait while the Socializer gains attention; and the fast-responding Mobilizer, though meticulous, prefers to check off boxes promptly while the free-spirited Socializer is spontaneous, moving quickly from one thought to another.

The Mobilizer is a Fast-Responding Demanding Extrovert

Positive Tendencies

Born leader
Confident
Decisive
Delegates
Dynamic
Embraces a challenge
Enthusiastic
Independent
Not easily discouraged
Organized
Results-oriented
Strong-willed

Negative Tendencies

Blunt
Bossy
Competitive
Controlling
Demands loyalty
Domineering
Impatient
Inflexible
Knows everything
May be rude, tactless
Quick-tempered

The Socializer is a Fast-Responding Engaging Extrovert

Positive Tendencies
Cheerful
Colorful dresser
Creative and colorful
Doesn't hold grudges
Enthusiastic
Makes friends quickly
Optimistic
People-oriented
Sense of humor
Spontaneous
Storyteller
Touchy-feely

Negative Tendencies
Disorganized
Doesn't listen
Easily distracted
Egotistical
Exaggerates
Forgetful
Loud
Overcommits
Overly talkative
Seeks social acceptance
Tends to arrive late
Undisciplined
Wants center stage

As you look over the Stabilizer and Organizer charts, notice how their tendencies overlap onto a linking personality as well. For example, the Stabilizer is easy going and the Organizer is thoughtful. These are similar traits, yet different. The Stabilizer will roll with the crowd to not make a fuss, while the Organizer is concerned whether the choice the crowd makes is safe for everyone.

Our amazing introverts, the Stabilizers and Organizers both keep to themselves for the most part. The Stabilizer is peacefully at home behind the scenes, keeping a steady pace and staying out of trouble. While the Organizer doesn't require the input of others to complete tasks, this introvert will share thoughts and opinions when asked. The Organizer dives into the details and research before giving an opinion. Similarly, the Stabilizer is fairly laid back and okay with others making decisions. Not easily ruffled, the Stabilizer says, "I'm fine," and truly means it.

The Stabilizer is a Slow-Responding Cautious Introvert

Positive Tendencies

Competent
Dry sense of humor
Easy going
Good listener
Good under pressure
Humble
Likes people
Patient
Quiet but witty
Relaxed and calm
Service-oriented
Supportive
Team player

Negative Tendencies

Fearful
Hides emotions
Indecisive
Indifferent
Judges
Low energy
May sleep a lot
Resists change
Stays uninvolved
Stubborn
Too compromising
Worried
Would rather watch

The Organizer is a Slow-Responding Thorough Introvert

Positive Tendencies

Analytical
Appreciates beauty
Compassionate
Creative
Detail-oriented
Economical
Faithful
High standards
Neat and tidy
Orderly
Self-disciplined
Serious
Tends to be right
Thoughtful
Uses charts, tables, and graphs

Negative Tendencies
Critical of others
Deep need for approval
Doesn't make friends easily
Hard to please
Holds back affection
Insecure socially
Internalizes guilt feelings
Low self-image
Moody
Perfectionistic
Standards too high
Too introspective
Withdrawn

As a reminder, this is a quick guide to the personalities and as such there may be more questions you want answered. Please don't hesitate to ask us questions; we love connecting with our readers. Check out the FAQ page in the back along with our contact information.

The Organizer dives into the details and research before giving an opinion.

Chapter 5
Heart Language

I (Rose) unpacked my suitcase and put my clothes away. As was usually the case when I went to writers conferences, about a fourth of my suitcase was filled with snacks. Who knew when I might get hungry, and I certainly didn't want to be out in the middle of nowhere with nothing wholesome to snack on. Once my suitcase was empty, I put it in the closet.

The next night my roommate and I decided we should have a snack after the evening keynote. We sat on our beds and discussed what was in the snack drawer. I pulled out one thing after another. Finally, I came to the snack mix. Both of us loved peanuts and chocolate and all the good stuff in the bag.

When I pulled them out of the drawer, I realized each bag of snack mix was labeled, one for me and one for my roommate. "Hmmm, wonder why these have our names on them?"

Small intentional actions make the biggest impact when connecting to your mate's heart language.

Candy, my roommate, opened hers and began eating her mix. "Yum, I really love raisins."

Raisins? I looked in my bag carefully. There wasn't a single raisin in my bag. Why?

My husband knew I really like snack mix but always took the raisins out because I don't care for them. When he packed the snacks, he removed all the raisins from my bag.

John knew I would be tired when I got back to the room after the evening program. He also knew that being an Organizer, I wouldn't start eating until I pulled all of the raisins from my bag and discarded them. Since he is a Mobilizer/Socializer, he wanted to make sure everything was just right for my trip and especially for the fellowship time in the evening. He knew my Organizer personality would be ready to rest and ignore all the other folks in our cabin. He thought he would encourage me to party just a little if I didn't have to pick the raisins out of my snack mix.

As an Organizer, it would be very easy for me to back into my shell and ignore everyone else during the times we weren't in meetings. But, thanks to my husband's encouragement and personal snack packing, I enjoyed a few minutes of fellowship with people I only saw once or twice a year.

Small intentional actions make the biggest impact when connecting to your mate's heart language.

Take a look at our Heart Language chart for a quick glance at how you can speak your mate's personality. stay close by and make sure you introduce your mate to all those around you.

Personality	Heart Language
	The Mobilizer wants to get things done. When you know your Mobilizer has a to-do list or a honey-do list, help get the items on the list checked off quickly. You will bring a smile to your spouse's face and maybe create time for a quick date! When communicating with your Mobilizer spouse, remember that the preferred method is short and to the point.
	Your Socializer's heart language is to have pure, uncomplicated fun. To please your Socializer spouse, plan outings where you can laugh and play with other people. Family outings and making good memories are a sweet spot for Socializers. If your heart language is not social, be sure to occasionally let yourself participate in your spouse's fun, relax, and enjoy the time together.
	Stabilizers feel secure when life is calm and peaceful. Preserve calm in the family, do what you can to restore peace, and give your Stabilizer spouse time alone to regroup and refresh. You may feel as though your Stabilizer spouse does a lot of nothing, which to you seems like a waste of time. Take time to just sit and be with your Socializer spouse and you will be speaking heart language.
	Organizers are not touchy-feely people so show your love for your spouse without being too physically demonstrative. Understand how your spouse likes things done and do them that way when you can. Your Organizer mate enjoys time spent with you or making a memory with the family. If you find yourself in a large group of people, remember your Organizer spouse is likely uncomfortable. So stay close by and make sure you introduce your mate to all those around you.

Here are actions you can use to speak your mate's heart language. Not all of these will work for everyone but choose the ones you think will be fun and add more to your list. Let us know of new ones that you discover.

If you notice your spouse seems overwhelmed, find a way to alleviate the stress by helping accomplish a task or two.

Coupons

Coupons used to be the highlight of the Sunday newspaper. No longer do we clip coupons, but we can tailor them to speak the heart language of your spouse.

Below are a few suggestions to make your spouse's day special.

Coupon: Good for a book lover's afternoon, lunch included. After lunch you are entitled to unlimited browsing in the bookstore of your choice. Book purchase included.

Coupon: Good for a candlelight dinner.

Coupon: Good for a dish pass when it is your turn to do the dishes.

Don't have time to make paper coupons? Create a text coupon. Just a few words, push the button, and you are done.

Message in a Bottle

It is so romantic to discover a message in a bottle. When you have an empty water bottle wash it well and remove the label. Put your message into the bottle, close it tightly, and float it in her bubble bath or his car wash bucket of water or slip it into the dishwasher just before unloading.

Pillowcases

When you will be away, use permanent markers to write a love note on a pillowcase. Cover your spouse's regular pillow with the new pillowcase and put in on the made bed just before you leave town. What a sweet bedtime surprise!

A heart language message well-timed and well-spoken is sure to bring a smile to even the most serious personality.

Lists

Lists make popular magazine articles so why not create your own article with a list of special things about your mate. A good place to start may be

10 Reasons I Love You

1. God created you just for me.

2. Our little girl looks like you.

3. You wrinkle your nose just before you smile.

4. You have cute legs.

5. You say it is endearing when I snort when I laugh.

6. You quit eating onions on your hamburgers because you know I don't like to smell them (or kiss you after you eat them!)

7. You take out the trash every day.

8. When I finish my dinner, you put my plate in the dishwasher.

9. You act like you are having fun no matter what we do.

10. You are the man/woman of my dreams.

Create lists for Valentine's Day, birthdays (Ten Reasons I'm Glad You Were Born), anniversaries (Top Five Reasons I'm Glad I Married You), and vacation days (Top Five Reasons I Would Go Anywhere With You), and for no occasion at all. Compile 365 Things I Love About You and your spouse can read one each day.

Special Signals

When we were children, we had all kinds of signals we used when we didn't want the parents to know what we were saying. Adapt that to your relationship with your mate and communicate in a way no one else in the room can interpret. For example, squeeze your mate's hand three times for "I love you" and four for "I love you too/more." Pull on one ear when you are ready to leave a party. Use your eyes when you want your mate to follow you to a specific place in the room. Raise one eyebrow when your mate is telling a story and it needs to be shortened or ended. You could also develop a way to text in code (maybe write the words backward) so only you knew what the message said.

Object Notes (Yes, guys, you can do this too!)

Briefcases, shoes, make up bags, work folders (these are on computer now), purses, and more make excellent mailboxes. Take a common object and make it the focus of your note.

Puzzle Piece

Note: When you are not with me there is a missing piece to my life.

Stick of Gum

Note: Let's always stick together.

Band Aid

No matter what is wrong, you always make me feel better.

Flashlight

Note: You are the light of my life.

Scripture Notes

Choose a verse of Scripture and briefly explain how it relates to you and your mate as a couple.

"But seek first his kingdom and his righteousness, and all these things will be given to you as well" (Matthew 6:33).

Note: I love coming down the steps every morning and seeing you spending time with God. It shows me you have your priorities in order. You lead our family so well.

"Love is patient, love is kind. It does not envy, it does not boast, it is not proud. It is not rude, it is not self-seeking, it is not easily angered, it keeps no record of wrongs. Love does not delight in evil but rejoices with the truth. It always protects, always trusts, always hopes, always perseveres" (1 Corinthians 13:4-7).

Note: You are real love to me.

"Look to the Lord and his strength; seek his face always" (1 Chronicles 16:11).

Note: I love your commitment to the Lord. It is comforting to me to know that you seek his face in everything you do and in all decisions regarding our family.

Pancake Notes

If pancakes are a favorite at your house, send a message of love to your spouse on his or her plate. This may seem like an activity that is more for the kids. However, try making a custom pancake for your spouse and see if it doesn't bring on a smile.

Draw a heart with the pancake batter. This is easily done by first making two small circles side by side and then adding a third circle underneath. When you lift the spoon from the third circle gently pull down to make a point.

Put a drop of red food coloring in a small amount of batter. Draw a heart on the griddle. Then cover the heart with a larger circle of a pancake. When you flip the pancake over, it will have a pink heart in the center of the pancake.

Does your spouse have a special interest? For your fisherman, draw a fish pancake for breakfast. Does your spouse like to read? Draw a book. Are you married to a golfer? Draw a golf club and ball.

Actions for Specific Personalities

Each personality has a different heart language and these suggestions will not work for every mate. But when you know the personality of your mate, you can tailor these activities and notes to speak directly to him or her.

For instance your Mobilizer mate will really enjoy occasional help checking something off their lists. If you notice your spouse seems overwhelmed, find a way to alleviate the stress by helping accomplish a task or two. This is the heart language of a Mobilizer.

Socializers are all about fun and people. Planning a surprise birthday party is a great way to speak to the heart of this mate. If you plan a surprise, be sure your Socializer has not planned a way to celebrate as well.

Your calm, quiet Stabilizer mate will appreciate your making a way to escape from the daily family chaos. Even fifteen minutes of quiet before dinner will refresh the Stabilizers and help them to enjoy family dinnertime more.

The Organizer mate often needs a break from a busy schedule of carpooling all day. Offering to do the noon pick up at school is a great word to the heart language of the Organizer. This personality may be thought of as a bit stodgy, but as the mate realize it is just the bent of the Organizer to withdraw from constant busyness and activity.

Whatever your spouse's personality remember your messages of love will be better received if spoken in the heart language familiar to your mate. Look for small ways to say "I love you" and "I care about you." A heart language message well-timed and well-spoken is sure to bring a smile to even the most serious personality.

Chapter 6
Champion Your Spouse

"I really love how Sam champions you, Linda," said Pastor David. "He is one of the most supportive husbands I've ever met. He keeps me posted about the success of your writing and speaking and lifts you up whenever we talk."

I (Goldie) couldn't hold back my tears as joy flooded my heart.

"Are you okay?"

"I'm good. It's just that I had no idea Sam talked about me," I blinked back more tears. "Thank you for letting me know." Truth be told, Sam had been my silent champion for years, and I never knew it.

Later that day I shared with Sam what Pastor had said and how it made me feel.

"Wow, really?" Sam folded the newspaper in his lap and looked up, "I always talk about you. Most of the time it's good," he chuckled.

To better know and meet the needs of our friends and family, we must first be willing to know ourselves.

"Just kidding, it's always good. I love you, Babe, and I'm proud of all you do."

In that moment I realized so much about my Organizer/Stabilizer husband. Because he's an internal processor, meaning he stores most of his emotions on the inside, I shouldn't be surprised that he would complement me in the same fashion.

As a double extrovert, Mobilizer/Socializer, I process everything externally, meaning you will know how I feel, when I feel it, no doubt about it. And I like to receive an atta-girl whenever they are handed out. Staying real.

Now let's take a look at how you can champion your spouse based on your personality strengths and your mate's emotional needs.

So far, you've

☑ discovered your dominant personality link and your personality smile, using one or both personality links on either side of yours. These combined links make up how you fully react or respond to others on a daily basis.

☑ said yes to descriptors in the "Behavior Identifiers" section.

☑ mentally checked off tendencies, both positive and negative, that are part of how you see yourself interacting with others.

☑ learned tangible ways to speak your mate's heart language.

What about day-to-day interactions?

Linking personalities spouse-to-spouse helps you discern small changes you can make to be a better champion of your spouse. Be aware, your mate may or may not be receptive to this new you. So go slow, don't expect huge changes on your spouses end and keep going.

Daily we choose to connect to the heart of our mates with hope, encouragement, adoration, respect, and tenderness. Or we choose to push down our mate's head with discouragement, ridicule, envy, apathy, and defeat. Our choices impact our relationship for better and for worse. Here are ways you can connect heart to heart in your marriage.

Mobilizers Connecting

With a Mobilizer Spouse

Release some control to keep some control, turning a possible tug-of-war into a reasonable give-and-take relationship. Both of you are born leaders and many relationships flourish with this combination when each party acknowledges their own weaknesses, instead of pointing out their mate's, and recognizes how the mate fills gaps with his or her strengths. Sometimes, the struggle for control distracts us from focusing on the bigger picture—why we said, "I do" in the first place.

A Mobilizer spouse recognizes the need to be in charge. Respect that feeling in your like-personality mate by offering a position of leadership instead of demanding to be in charge of everything. Establish a division of mutual responsibilities rather than a delegation of you do this and I'll do that. Remember, your life together is a partnership.

Respect goes a long way with this personality connection. As a wife, I (Goldie) choose to respect my husband's position as head of our home. He is quick to get my thoughts when we're making decisions that impact our family or just the two of us. I speak up for sure, yet knowing the buck has to stop somewhere, I default to him in making the final decision. This is mutually satisfying. I know my opinion matters and he's respected—win, win.

Heart to Heart: Appreciation goes a long way with Mobilizers. Take every opportunity to show, not tell, your spouse how much their actions mean to you.

With a Socializer Spouse

Having a Socializer spouse can be the most fantastic adventure you've ever experienced. Until you realize, every day seems to be a party. As a Mobilizer you want to accomplish your goals/tasks/projects in the fastest and most efficient way possible. Your Socializer mate has an easier time staying engaged in projects and tasks when there is an element of fun involved. If you don't provide the fun your mate most likely will.

For your Socializer, sharing is caring. Your Socializer mate loves listening to and telling stories. Give him or her time to share what happened during their day. When you share about your day, turn your typical bullet points and one-word answers into a couple of sentences. When the opportunity arises, give your mate a glimpse into your heritage by sharing fun facts about your family. Both of you enjoy competition. As much as you like to win or be the best, your Socializer spouse likes being in the spotlight. Every time you speak well of your spouse to others, you shine the spotlight on the one you love.

Recognize your Socializer's enthusiasm and energy as a plus. Being a glass half-full personality is not bad, but when the glass is completely empty or broken, your mate's tendency is to go from high-energy drama to bottom-of-the-pit trauma in a heartbeat. Now is not the time to criticize or say, "What happened to miss (or mister) happy-go-lucky?" Instead, offer a hug. Listen sincerely to the many details your Stabilizer needs to tell you, and then—don't try to fix it. Instead, ask, "What can I do that would help?"

Heart to Heart: Always applaud your Socializer mate's creativity.

With a Stabilizer Spouse

Stabilizers may have to be coaxed into participating as active members of the family. A few warm and fuzzy words go a long way. Though quiet, they thrive on recognition and verbal encouragement. Your Stabilizer mate likes to be with family but sometimes retreats to solitude to recharge those introvert batteries. Assure your Stabilizer you understand their preference to temporarily step away from the gathering.

A Stabilizer mate is a natural peacemaker and tends to go along with what you ask to make you happy. This often leads Stabilizers to take on many roles which leads to overload. Think slow and steady. Let your Stabilizer spouse know ahead of time what's on your calendar, and what's expected relevant to calendar events. Stabilizers do not like surprises. Ask about your spouse's scheduling plans and preferences. You may often hear, "Nothing planned. I'm good."

Your Stabilizer spouse can be easily stressed or overwhelmed by your do-it-now mannerism. Be intentionally aware of your spouse's need for time to ponder and problem-solve as part of the Stabilizer's process of completing the job.

Heart to Heart: Respect your Stabilizer mate's need for peace.

With an Organizer Spouse

Organizers process slowly and internally. Organizers can be easily overwhelmed by the naturally boisterous and powerful Mobilizer. Sensitive to the needs of others and loyal to fault, the Organizer may be found tending to the needs of someone outside the family; a tendency the Mobilizer may consider a waste of energy.

Ask a question and allow a few seconds, or even minutes, for your mate to process the answer. Quick to listen and slow to speak, the Organizer investigates and typically shares accurate information. Given unpressured time, Organizers produce details, not fairytales. Given time, Organizers have excellent organizational and time management skills and are helpful at keeping others on track. Ask your Organizer mate's opinions for work and home. This introvert won't necessarily speak up without prompting but enjoys being involved in family and group activities.

Your Organizer spouse will rarely ask for recognition, but deep down yearns for appreciation. Praise is not something you give naturally, so make an effort to genuinely recognize what your spouse does for your home and family.

Heart to Heart: Acknowledge and applaud your spouse's way of wanting to follow the rules, even if it seems a bit much.

Socializers Connecting

With a Mobilizer Spouse

Remember, Mobilizers are get-to-the-point, no-nonsense people who want to finish tasks as efficiently as possible and move on to the next item on their lists. Your Mobilizer spouse wants the facts in three bullet points rather than listening to a lengthy discussion. Your Mobilizer mate appreciates an occasional story, told factually with minimal embellishment. Though short-winded conversations are not natural to a Socializer, your Mobilizer greatly appreciates the condensed version.

A Socializer can get caught up in the drama of a situation. Mobilizers give full attention to problem solving. Communicate with your Mobilizer by sharing the major points, where you feel stuck, and where you need help. Avoid over-explaining beyond the need-to-know information. Listen to the Mobilizer's recommendations and repeat what you heard. Follow through and let the Mobilizer know how those suggestions solved the problem. Showing genuine respect and appreciation for your Mobilizer spouse is priceless.

As a Socializer, you're a creative, out of the box thinker. Encourage your Mobilizer mate by sharing with him some of your creative solutions to his problems. Showing an interest in his tasks opens the window of reciprocation on his behalf. You never know, he may even sit down and watch a show you like.

Heart to Heart: Communicate your appreciation and respect to your Mobilizer. Invite this hard worker to rest, refresh, and join you on a spontaneous adventure.

With a Socializer Spouse

Socializers thrive on center stage. There are natural challenges when two Socializers get together, both vie for the attention of those around them. This can lead into one-upmanship leaving one or both feeling left out. For social events, alternate being the designated driver; drive the jokes, drive the conversation, drive the crowd. Use a tag team approach. Invite your mate into the conversation. Create a signal letting your mate know you want to jump into the conversation. Allow your spouse adequate time to share a story, get a few laughs, and be the spotlight. Be careful not to interrupt and steal your spouse's story.

Agree ahead of time on who will be responsible for tasks in the home. Bills, chores, and cleaning are not usually the fun jobs in a relationship, but the two of you can make any situation enjoyable. Encourage each other throughout the month to complete all the tasks and celebrate accomplishing small and big goals together.

Heart to Heart: Create a time during the week for you to focus on your spouse.

With a Stabilizer Spouse

 Your Stabilizer mate's calm and cool personality can help you remain grounded in moments of high drama or low trauma. You both enjoy being around people yet respond differently to the other personalities. Your Stabilizer spouse retreats from conflict rather than entering into family brouhaha. Stabilizers prefer quiet activities and time spent in individual study.

This personality tends to internalize thoughts. When you pose a challenge or question give your Stabilizer adequate time to contemplate and consider an answer, this often yields the positive results you desire.

Some may look upon their Stabilizer spouse as lazy. But being thoughtful and laid back should not be confused with being lethargic. Stabilizers are rejuvenated by their naps, especially after a long day at the office. Before inviting your spouse into another activity give your mate a chance to recoup.

Heart to Heart: Encourage your Stabilizer to participate in fun activities, but don't demand it.

With an Organizer Spouse

Don't rush your Organizer to answer. Organizers think through every response and process all new information before they speak. Give them time to do so. You're spontaneous while your Organizer is methodical. Social events requiring them to make an immediate decision can result in an embarrassing moment for your mate and no one wants that.

Organizers live at a different pace than you. Humor simmers at a slower speed for this personality. While fun comes easily for you, remember Organizers have to work at having a good time.

Organizer spouses are sensitive, so be clear in your expectations to ensure no misunderstandings occur between the two of you. If you make a comment intended to be facetious or meant in a different way, watch the face of your Organizer mate to make sure it was received as intended. Speak slowly, especially if you're excited. This helps your Organizer to grasp your concepts.

Heart to Heart: Occasionally invite your Organizer to join in karaoke or dance. Deep down they want to join in but are hesitant to say so.

Stabilizers Connecting

With a Mobilizer Spouse

 Your goal-oriented Mobilizer can create stress unintentionally. Anxious to reach a goal, the Mobilizer moves forward in the most direct way possible. As the Stabilizer, you're glad to see your spouse accomplish a goal, but it's difficult to move at the same speed. When working on projects or household tasks, look for ways to help your Mobilizer meet goals. Remind your mate you can meet a deadline when given enough notice.

Mobilizers like being in charge. This strong personality says *I love you* by accomplishing tasks that move the relationship forward. Your Mobilizer can be a beneficial source for good ideas. If you have something you want done ask your Mobilizer for input. If by chance your spouse does everything in bulldozer fashion, preface your conversation with, "I'd like your input, but I don't need you to fix it." This puts a Mobilizer at ease and more receptive to listening.

Be direct in conversations with your Mobilizer spouse. Keep what you say short and to the point. Mobilizers think fast and act fast, so long-winded conversation is not the best approach.

Heart to Heart: Show appreciation to your Mobilizer throughout the week.

With a Socializer Spouse

Your fun-loving Socializer never meets a stranger. You both like people, but you don't do as well in large crowds unless you know a majority of the attendees. Ask your outgoing mate to introduce you to one new person at social events. Take time during the commute to consider a few conversation starters you feel comfortable with.

Stabilizers are exhausted by the time they get home from work, yet your Socializer spouse is ready to head out the door or dive into conversation. One way to look forward to your after-hours time together is to be preemptive. Tell your Socializer, "I really like how spontaneous you are and your eagerness to share with me everything that has happened in your day." Give your spouse a minute to say thank you. Then you can say, "Do you know what makes me happy?"

Don't be surprised if your question is met with a quick fun response or lack of response. In fact, take a moment and giggle with your mate or gaze into your spouses' eyes reassuringly and say, "It's when I can come home from work and have fifteen minutes to unwind before heading out the door or jumping into a conversation. I appreciate you and want to give you my full attention, and I can do that better when I've had a moment to shut down and (close my eyes or take a shower or insert your answer here). Can you help make that happen?"

By doing this, you're able to speak truth and give a solution, which is helpful to Socializers.

Heart to Heart: Listen intently when your Socializer tells a story and then share your favorite part.

With a Stabilizer Spouse

 Stabilizers take time to prepare for and complete tasks, which has pros and cons. The pro is you have an easy-going outlook on life, and the con, tasks are uncompleted because neither of you took the initiative to get it done. An easy help is to post a planner in the open, then use two colors to designate who is responsible for completing what. Set timers throughout the week as audible reminders and reward yourselves with an evening curled up on the couch watching your favorite movies.

You truly understand each other and your need for a peaceful home environment. Being together is a time of refreshment and oasis. A word of caution here, it's easy to get into a rut when both of you are laid back. Create a *Joy Jar*. Take a few minutes to write things you'd like to do together on slips of paper, drop the slips in the jar, and draw one out when the mood hits.

Heart to Heart: Give your Stabilizer consistent words of encouragement.

With an Organizer Spouse

Organizers appreciate your universal love of people and your desire to see others succeed. As you present different perspectives on subjects, your Organizer mate will interject questions as a result of processing each of them. Don't take an Organizer's questioning as criticism, step back a moment and appreciate your spouse's desire to fully understand and fully process what you bring up in conversation. Most Organizers are natural researchers. They can uncover information you may not be aware of. This is a good thing.

Your Organizer tends to be a perfectionist. Don't belittle this trait. Recognize your mate as a person of excellence with words of affirmation. Because of this perfectionist attribute, Organizers take more time than others to complete tasks so encourage your mate along the way.

Heart to Heart: Appreciate the sensitivity of your Organizer mate.

Organizers Connecting

With a Mobilizer Spouse

Mobilizers share your attention to detail but not your desire for perfection. When discussing plans, your mate's fast track to the finish line may overpower your need for deep thinking before you move forward. Don't be alarmed, be forearmed. Since Mobilizers take on the challenge to fix everything be prepared to ask your mate's opinion on the plan and to include relational boundaries, preferably as bullet points.

Relational Boundary Phrases

- I feel loved when I'm not rushed.
- I like to know ahead of time what the plans are.
- I like to be involved in making plans.

Use the following phrases to encourage your Mobilizer.

- I trust your opinions.
- I'm with you all the way.
- You're not alone.

As an Organizer, you can be overly sensitive. Don't let the abrupt manner of your Mobilizer mate make you feel inadequate, unimportant, or wrong in the way you deal with life. Though your spouse can learn to be gentler, bossy remarks shouldn't be taken personally.

Heart to Heart: Applaud your Mobilizer's ability to complete new activities.

With a Socializer Spouse

Organizers tend to roll their eyes at the energy and playfulness of Socializers. Instead, choose to relax and appreciate your mate's propensity for fun; you may find life more joyful. On the other hand, if you are the brunt of one of your Socializer's jokes, you can easily get your feelings hurt. To spare you some pain and your mate some guilt, get in front of the joke telling. Tell your spouse, "When I'm made fun of, I feel unloved." This simple statement of truth can speak volumes to your Socializer. Lengthy details of why it makes you feel unloved shuts this spouse down as does accusatory tones and references. Therefore, keep your thoughts short and sweet.

As the Organizer, you benefit greatly when your Socializer helps with parties and social gatherings. The Socializer's energy and creative processing carries over into every experience and helps others get excited when they may not ordinarily do so. Step back from having a perfect event and embrace an event everyone will enjoy attending, including you.

As an Organizer, you thrive on time alone. If you find yourself being short with your spouse, take a look at how much time and energy you have been expending. Perhaps, you need to retreat to your bedroom or under a big shade tree in the backyard to recharge your batteries.

Heart to Heart: Say yes more often when your Socializer wants to party.

With a Stabilizer Spouse

Organizers and Stabilizers enjoy alone time. However, you may not want alone time at the same time. If there're chores to be done, your Stabilizer may want to rest before and after and this could rub you the wrong way. Be aware and include rest in your schedule.

Don't overwhelm your Stabilizer with too many decisions at one time. If you have a must-get-done list of tasks, let your mate know in advance your desire to work on some of them over the weekend. Be sure you've allotted plenty of time for your spouse to contemplate which path will be taken to accomplish the task. Supply a preferred deadline. Don't rush. Don't push.

Stabilizers are fairly easy going and don't often voice inflexible opinions. Therefore, ask your mate's opinion more often and listen attentively to the answers.

Heart to Heart: Say thank you more often to your Stabilizer.

With an Organizer Spouse

Two Organizers running a home can work well together because you agree on many things. You both love attention to detail and cherish times of deep research, so expect long stretches of silence as you gaze across the room in muted bliss. Misunderstandings occur when the lines of obligation are blurry. Make sure both of you know what's expected of each other with chore assignments and such. Organizers love details and dislike surprises. A chore chart to use for the family is a good way to make sure everyone knows what is expected of them.

The perfectionist aspect of your Organizer personalities could create conflict of whose way is the right way to perform a task or finish a job. Before issues become challenges, work with your Organizer spouse, highlight what's needed to reach the goals you've both set and divide the tasks to accomplish them in the allotted time.

Heart to Heart: Choose more often to tell your Organizer, "You're right!"

Take the time to read about all the personalities in this section not just your own, as this will help you identify and engage better with others. Now let's get to navigating the tough times, personality-wise.

Chapter 7
Navigate Tough Times

As an Organizer, I (Rose), take much longer than my Mobilizer/Socializer husband to process difficulties. For me, almost every situation has an emotional aspect to it. So, when I finally accept and deal with a hard situation, I am usually left with the lingering emotions. On the other hand, my Mobilizer husband just wants to fix things as quickly as he can. He is happy to have people come to help and wants to move on.

Understanding personality can make a huge difference during times of loss, special situations, or stress.

For example, when my mother died, I was a young mom with three small children. Just the day-to-day duties were overwhelming. In the midst of my grief, I could not even think of what to fix for dinner, much less how to get the children from place to place or help them with their homework. Some of it I had to do and I went through the motions. The job got done but I know I didn't do a very good job.

My husband realized how difficult this time period was for me and stepped up to the plate. He took over everything he could during the time he was not at work. On his way home from work, he picked up dinner so I didn't have to think about it. Bottom line was he did everything he could to let me process my grief and get through it in my own way. It was a positive situation for both of us because I had time to be alone when I needed to and my Mobilizer, Mr. Fix-It, husband was doing what he could to fix it.

Every marriage has times when situations occur that are less than what we would like. Disappointments come. Losses work their way into our lives. Family members act or react inappropriately. Children's problems become our own.

Even the strongest marriages have rough spots, many of which are prompted by something or someone other than the marriage partners. Most of these spots catch us by surprise. We never see them coming. But if we are continually working to make our marriages stronger and drawing closer to one another and to God, we can face difficult situations that arise with peace and confidence. Knowledge of the personalities is a bonus in these times.

Here are a few situations that may occur over the course of your marriage.

Loss of a Loved One

No matter what your age when you marry, it probably won't be long after you walk down the aisle that you find yourself at the graveside of someone you love – a parent, grandparent, or great grandparent. Times of loss of a loved one are stressful and the normal that had been your lifestyle since you were married is no more. You and your family have to create a new normal for yourselves as a couple and for your family.

Death of a Child

No one should have to bury a child. It just doesn't seem to follow the correct order of life and death when a couple finds themselves at the graveside of their child. Many children are lost each year through accidents, miscarriage, disease, etc. Often these deaths are sudden and unexpected. Grasping the fact that your child has gone to heaven prematurely is something you will probably never get over. But you must trust God that His plan for that child did not include longevity.

Loss of a Job

When a husband or wife loses a job, a financial gap is created, self-confidence slumps, and you must adjust to a new way of life. The spouse who has lost a job doesn't know what to do and the job hunt goes back to the beginning for that person. Many decisions have to be made such as whether or not to get a new job, whether to pursue a new career which may involve going back to school to develop expertise in a new area, whether or not to move to another part of the country if an opportunity arises, and so forth.

Financial Difficulties

Not all financial difficulties come from loss of a job. Many times the hardships in this area come from situations out of the couple's control. A disabled child who requires extra care and multiple specialists can be taxing to the budget. Whether by birth or as the result of an accident, a disabled child in the home adds to the responsibilities of all other family members. Special schools, therapists, and multiple doctor visits prevail. Increased duties around the house create little time for rest for the parents. When we are tired, we become stressed much quicker and that affects everything we do in our homes.

An Illness of the Wife or Husband

When one or the other of a married couple becomes sick and cannot help with household duties, it puts physical strain on the other. Depending on the age of the couple, stress may be caused by a change in finances, inability to travel, increased doctor's appointments, and so forth. Concern about losing a mate creeps in and anxiety over how the surviving mate will be able to live alone is present.

Navigating by Personality

This list, though not comprehensive, gives us enough examples upon which to base how each personality has its own way to deal with tough times.

Each personality has its own way of dealing with stress and difficulty. A few of the ways you may deal with stress based on your personality follow.

Because Mobilizers want to get things done, you will probably deal with stress the same way you deal with everything else, very matter-of-factly. Your personality will focus on finding a solution to every problem no matter how difficult. Even in a highly emotional situation, you want to fix it. If, however, your spouse is a more sensitive personality, you may need to work extra hard not to become impatient and overbearing. You have probably thought in stressful situations, "Oh, just get over it." This is not as easy for other personalities as it is for you. You also need to remember that every problem doesn't have an easy 1-2-3 solution. Some situations require quite a bit of work to get through them and it may take time to recover.

Even the strongest marriages have rough spots, many of which are prompted by something or someone other than the marriage partners.

Each personality processes grief and loss in a specific way. If you are the strong Mobilizer, look at others who are experiencing the same loss. Is there some way you can pick up the slack and help them process their grief? Can you make a plan that satisfies your yen for control but is relaxed enough for even the laid back Stabilizer personality?

Because Socializers outwardly express their emotions, you may find your method of dealing with loss is more people-oriented than other personalities. When you are hurting or upset about something, you need your "peeps" surrounding you with love and attention. You hurt and grieve just like you do anything else. You put one hundred percent into it and, unlike your Stabilizer and Organizer friends, want to talk about your loss. Remember when your fellow Socializer friends are grieving for any reason, they need you more than ever to demonstrate that you care for them.

Other personalities may think Socializers are not taking the grieving/loss process seriously. That is not true. Like every personality, Socializers have their own way of dealing with the loss. You must process your loss and for you, it takes a lot of friends to help you do that. Just remember, as we pointed out about the Mobilizer, don't expect everyone around you to process it in the same way.

Because Stabilizers like to hide their emotions, they may not seem as open during the grieving process as others. During these times, the Stabilizers need others to respect their desire to be unemotional about their loss, even though they feel deeply. They are also practical and want to make sure things that need to be done get done. Because at times of loss there tend to be lots of people around, often that can tire the Stabilizer. He or she will need to escape from the crowd from time to time as processing continues.

If your spouse is a Stabilizer, remember they do not like to grieve openly. Give them the understanding to know they can proceed at their own pace. Don't insist they approach special situations just like you do. Grieve together but understand that the method might be different.

Organizers face special situations quietly, not always wanting to be open about their feelings. However, Organizers are very sensitive and feel very deeply. They often take longer to process loss because of their sensitivity. It may take Organizers a while to verbalize feelings over a difficult situation. Often added to their stress over the situation is the stress of having to be in crowds of people who want to help. Organizers need to be sure in the midst of stress to pull aside and rest. Crowds of extra people in the house increase this personality's need to have some time to themselves.

If your mate is an Organizer, respect his or her need for solitude. You may have to "run interference" in order to create some time to recharge. Keep in mind that during times of loss and difficulty, your personality may be energized by your need to get things taken care of, but your Organizer or Stabilizer mate will need extra rest.

Understanding personality can make a huge difference during times of loss, special situations, or stress. Knowing how you and your mate will react and how you process your inner feelings will let you know how you can be most helpful and supportive during difficult times.

Chapter 8
He Thinks, She Thinks

We encourage all couples to come together at least twice a month for a "He Thinks, She Thinks" time of sharing your thoughts. "He Thinks, She Thinks" is a calendared time to breathe in deep thoughts you've pondered and share everything that's happening on your side of the bed. This is the time to share your struggles during the past couple weeks, your joyful moments, your short-term desires and far off dreams. But no worries, this isn't a free-for-all that lasts for hours, we suggest a flexible thirty to forty-five-minute structure every personality can agree to.

A negative word spoken in the heat of the moment can be diffused if our desire is to thrive in our marriages.

Each of us come to a marriage with habits and tendencies of a single person. We've found to better know and meet the needs of our friends and family, we must first be willing to know ourselves.

As we understand more about our personalities, specifically our knee jerk tendencies, we can help our spouses understand how he or she can care for our emotional needs better with a few simple techniques.

Get In Front of It – As you discover your spouse's less than desirable actions, phrases, and habits, you know, those little things that drive you crazy and use this technique to prevent a spring shower from developing into a thunderstorm.

Write down the unwanted feelings pain points, your spouse's actions stir up that fit this starter statement, "I'm not sure if your knew this, but, when I'm (excluded, made fun of, ignored, fill in the blank) it makes me feel (insert your pain point)."

Pain Points: Unworthy. Lonely. Unloved. Rejected. Add your own.

This technique can also be a conversation starter to help your spouse understand, without direct confrontation, how the words and actions of others impact you. You can use this technique to get in front of pain points to help friends and family members understand you better as well. Encourage them to do the same.

> Sometimes you have to let go of difficulties in order to grow as a couple.

Diffuse It – Tempers can flare without warning. You can see the kettle starting to bubble before the water is even warm. This technique is for those moments. A negative word spoken in the heat of the moment can be diffused if our desire is to thrive in our marriages.

"If I hear you say how your mom makes spaghetti different than me one more time, I'll explode!"

Yeah. Where do you go from here?

Step back. Don't justify yourself. Take a breath. And say, "I'm sorry. Comparing you to my mom or anyone else is not right. Please forgive me."

Key Words: I'm sorry. You're right. Please forgive me.

Make the Most of It – Sometimes you have to let go of difficulties in order to grow as a couple. Ask yourself, "How can I come alongside my spouse in this moment to help him get through (losing his job, being criticized, etc. Insert the situation)."

Your answer may be something like these:

Stay silent.

Give him a hug.

Pray.

Sit and listen.

Take on part of the burden.

Make a phone call.

No matter the situation, we always have a better choice to make and when we choose to make the choice based on how it will help our spouse, it's most often the best choice.

Lasting Links for Couples

As we conclude our guide to maximizing heart connections, here are a few final words of personality-specific encouragement.

Mobilizer Mate

Speak with love and a bit of gentleness.

Smile more often.

Champion your mate with boldness and courage.

Ask for help, even when you can do it yourself.

Remember—Making a list for yourself is great, but let your spouse make their own.

Socializer Mate

Curb your spontaneity by focusing more on your spouse.

Express your love with genuineness and sincerity.

Keep your spouse's best interests at heart and persevere through tough times.

Help your mate view life not so much as a party but as a constant source of joy.

Remember—Have fun, but never at the expense of your spouse.

Stabilizer Mate

Patience is one of your strengths to show off.

Stretch yourself and volunteer to help your spouse around the house.

Champion calmly and with love.

Find a friend so you can encourage one another.

Remember—Your calm, non-confrontational personality can be an anchor in your home.

Organizer Mate

Cultivate couple friendships with your spouse's friends.

Love your spouse by outwardly showing it.

Don't impose your perfectionist tendencies on your spouse.

Consider occasionally overstepping the boundaries to create a little fun.

Remember—Organizers are great mates especially when they smile more often.

Chapter 9
Before "I Do"

Before John and I (Rose) married, we knew we needed to get to know one another better. There was only one problem. We lived about 1500 miles apart. Since we weren't able to really date and go out for long, romantic dinners, we spent most of our getting-to-know-you time either on the phone (yes, one that had a cord) or writing letters (yes, real letters that you had to put a stamp on). Engaged couples of today would probably scoff at those antiquated ways of preparing for marriage. But we truly were able to know our thoughts and feelings about situations because we thought them through and discussed them.

Had we known and understood the personalities during those years, I am sure we would have applied that knowledge to each discussion. But when we studied the personalities later, we had a good foundation of knowing how the other thought and how every situation would be processed.

Now that we have studied personalities, we agree it would have been a wonderful thing to have known before we were married. But since we didn't have that option, we laid the foundation by spending lots of time getting to know one another.

In our country divorce statistics have risen for a long time. Therefore, it seems wise to do your "homework" before you step up to the altar. That homework could include getting to know each other better through understanding the personality of your mate-to-be. If you have gotten this far in the book and you are not yet married, you must know the knowledge here in the book is valuable in your relationship. The time you spend studying personalities and addressing your differences and similarities will pay off in a big way as your relationship deepens.

You have probably noticed that you and your fiancé are different in many ways. You do not necessarily have the same strengths. Often you are drawn to someone who is different because you like the way he or she is strong in areas where you are weak and vice versa.

No matter how long your engagement is, there is never enough time to learn everything about another person. But the engagement time can be time well spent if you look at it as an important time of getting to know one another. Take time to converse and tell each other about your childhood

No matter how long your engagement is, there is never enough time to learn everything about another person.

and family memories. According to bestselling author and professor of psychology at Northwest University, Dr. Les Parrott, one of the best questions you can ask yourself during this time is, "Would I like to be married to me?" That one soul-searching question will cause you to think deeply about yourself and your personality.

Every relationship is unique and the way you relate to your fiancé will not be the same way that other couples relate. Several factors enable couples to learn, grow, and live at peace with one another. A few of those are

1) They understand each other. Personality knowledge can help with that.

2) They know how they and their mates act and react. Personality knowledge can help with that.

3) They know themselves and feel good about who they are. Personality knowledge can help with that.

4) They are not easily offended. Personality knowledge can help with that.

5) They do not hold grudges. Personality knowledge can help with that.

6) They want to have a healthy marriage and put a high priority on that. Personality knowledge can help with that.

7) They must sometimes put the other first. Personality knowledge can help with that.

8) They know a happy family takes a lot of work. Personality knowledge can help with that.

There is some truth in the adage "Opposites attract" and that is one reason why understanding the personality of your spouse is imperative for your marriage to thrive. Take a look at Doug and his fiancée Hannah.

Doug and Hannah were planning to get married often sitting and talking with each other for hours. They had studied the personalities and determined that Doug was a Mobilizer and Hannah was an Organizer. In other words, their personalities were very different. Once they began planning their wedding, their distinct differences came into play. The first thing Doug did was make a list of the things that needed to be done. Hannah started reading down the list but had a hard time getting past the first item – "Secure romantic outdoor space." Hannah had dreamed of getting married by a lake ever since she was a little girl. She wanted to process her thoughts about each item, not just hurriedly cross them off the list for the sake of a checkmark.

At first, Mobilizer Doug became impatient because Hannah was taking so long. But given just a few minutes of thought, he remembered Organizers like to process things as they go and before they speak. He tried to be a little less anxious to get things checked off and a bit more sensitive to

Hannah's need to process. The planning may have taken a little longer this way but Doug and Hanna understood the need to work together. In the end both of them accepted the other's position and the wedding was planned in a way that everyone was happy.

Marley and Chandler had a similar planning experience. Marley's Socializer personality was a little harder to resolve with Chandler's Stabilizer one.

Marley wanted to invite everyone she knew (and some she didn't) so they could have a great big celebration. Her Socializer personality loved a party. Having a room full of people to honor them on their wedding day was as much a part of the day to Marley as were the flowers, the cake, and other things. However, Chandler never felt comfortable in a big crowd, especially when he was the center of attention. He couldn't really understand Marley's love of a crowd of people. Chandler had several really close friends, but they were all in the wedding party. So other than his family, he felt like there would be plenty of his favorite people at the wedding.

This couple had to find a way to compromise so that each felt like their big day was the way they wanted it. Knowing their personalities were different, Marley and Chandler discussed how many people would it really take to make Marley feel like "Queen for the Day." Chandler expressed his dislike of crowds but felt if the number of guests wasn't too big, he could handle it. Marley planned short breaks throughout the day so Chandler would enjoy their special day, too. They made a few other compromises to make sure neither felt uncomfortable or slighted on their big day.

There are probably hundreds of scenarios where one personality marries another and from the pre-marital days they realize it will take work for their marriage to be successful. All marriages take work. It's just that some personality combinations require more work than others. If both individuals in the couple are willing from the start to do the necessary work to make it happen, it won't be as hard. Willingness to make a marriage work is part of the equation for a successful marriage. When you discover why your mate acts and reacts as they do, you will understand how you can temper your reaction to situations that will help you get through them smoothly.

Psalm 133:1 says, "How good and pleasant it is when God's people live together in unity!" Living together in unity is something that all married couples need to strive for. Just loving your spouse is not enough to ensure your marriage will thrive. Knowing the personality of your mate gives you information that can help you work through conflict, make plans that are satisfying to all the family, and live together in harmony.

If you are talking about marriage, we urge you to take time to discuss important things with each other before you say "I do." Here are some questions you can start with. As you are talking, don't hesitate to vocalize anything that comes to mind during the discussion.

Questions for pre-marital discussions.

What were your childhood goals and dreams?

What goals and dreams do you have for our marriage?

Do you have goals that will affect our marriage?

Are you willing to compromise personal goals for our marriage?

Where do you see us in five years?

How will we approach problems?

What are your strengths? What are mine? How can these work together?

Do you want to have children? Why or why not?

How many children do you want to have?

How do you see God in your everyday life?

How important is it for you to pray?

Do you squeeze the tube of toothpaste or roll it up?

Appendix

FAQ

Here are a few frequently asked questions for the Two Lindas.

Q-I am already married. I'm not sure I really understood my mate until I read this book. Now that I understand personalities, it makes sense why we have such a hard time getting along. What can we do to grow our relationship in the midst of frequent squabbles?

A-This book has given you great tools to grow your marriage. If you and your mate are having trouble getting along, perhaps it is because of a lack of personality knowledge. Read through the book again together. Stop at places that one of you doesn't understand and discuss it. Discuss parts where you see your spouse. If you have an "aha" moment, stop and talk about the time that knowledge would have helped the situation.

Perhaps your mate is a strong Socializer personality. He or she just can't understand why you don't like to have fun and party all the time. As a strong Organizer, your kind of fun is different from your mate's. As you read the book together, don't turn the page until you have fully discussed every little difference. Find ways you can create dates you both will enjoy. Agree from the beginning of the book to be honest about your feelings and to do your best to help your mate understand you.

Q-At what age does a person's personality become obvious to others?

A-Personality can be determined at a very young age. Once you are aware of the characteristics of the different personalities, you realize some traits begin to exhibit themselves in infancy and toddlerhood. Therefore, your spouse has been developing his or her personality for a long time. He or she cannot change his or her reactions overnight. You have probably heard stories of your mate as he or she grew up and how his or her personality exhibited itself at an early age.

If you have children, you have observed your children at play. I'm sure you've noticed some play together well and some don't. The way they play is telling. Sarah dumps her blocks out in a pile by turning the bucket over. Robby takes each block out of the bucket one by one and strategically places them on the floor. Rebecca arranges hers in a creative pattern while, Justin, doesn't seem to care how they are arranged. Based on their God-given nature, children are Mobilizers, Socializers, Stabilizers, and Organizers.

Marriage works the same way. The only difference is blocks have turned into adult responsibilities and actions and reactions are often stronger than when you were children because of that responsibility.

Q- How does your faith fit with personalities?

A-We love this question. Actually, we are thinking about writing a quick guide specifically about this subject. Both of us are Christians and as such, we researched the Bible and wise teachings by trustworthy believers before we even started our journey into studying the personalities.

Our findings show we are created by design to be productive based on how we were created. Both of us have distinctly different personalities, yet, the same faith. This helps us write in unity, because knowing about our personality strengths and weaknesses we hold up each other's arms when needed.

Q-My mate and I are the same personalities. How does understanding the personalities impact our daily lives?

A-Many times like personalities have similar reactions toward life events. So if you and your mate are both Mobilizer personalities, you have a greater understanding of how your mate must feel when he or she loses his or her job, walks through the death of a friend, or opens a box containing his or her first published book. In the case of a difficult life situation, you are the best person to empathize and walk alongside him or her through this.

Q-Everyday, we talk with people, whether in person or through technology. Think about the miscommunication that occurs when we speak. Most of it can be eliminated if we speak to the personality instead of the person. How can personality knowledge impact miscommunication?

A-Speaking to the personality of the person helps me. As a Mobilizer, I curb my reactions so

I can consider a better path instead of my gut impression. I take a breath (albeit a second or two) and allow a response to come out, based on who they are and who I am, instead of words that could possibly ignite hurt feelings. On the other hand, if you are an Organizer, you think before you speak and take time to choose your words carefully.

Q-Why is it important to consider the other person first? Shouldn't they be responsible for their actions?

A-God instructs us to love others as we love ourselves. Therefore, considering the way another individual receives you is important in linking together with who they are. The seconds it takes to think of others first will save you and them a lifetime of conflict.

Assessment Key

	Mobilizer	Socializer	Stabilizer	Organizer
1	a	b	d	c
2	a	b	d	c
3	c	a	d	b
4	d	c	a	b
5	b	a	d	c
6	c	a	d	b
7	c	a	d	b
8	d	b	a	c
9	c	b	d	a
10	c	d	b	a
11	d	a	b	c
12	a	b	d	c
13	a	d	c	b
14	d	a	c	b
15	d	a	c	b
16	b	c	a	d
17	b	d	c	a
18	a	d	b	c
19	c	b	d	a
20	a	b	d	c
21	a	b	d	c
22	c	a	d	b
23	d	c	b	a
24	b	d	c	a
25	a	d	c	b
26	a	d	b	c
Total				
	Mobilizer	Socializer	Stabilizer	Organizer

Acknowledgments

The *LINKED* *for Couples Quick Guide to Personalities* is book four in our LINKED* series. Acknowledgments are never complete without recognizing the direction of the Creator of all. Thank you for entrusting us with a love of people and their personalities. Thank You, God, for the opportunity to be Your messengers.

To Bold Vision Books. What a blessing to work with such a professional team to whom only excellence will do. Thank you, George and Karen Porter and your team for believing this project can change lives. We agree.

Our families are our head cheerleaders. We love you and appreciate you. The sacrifices you have made for the writing of this book series have not gone unnoticed. Thank you to our parents who modeled to us how a godly family grows together and supports one another.

To our editors. Your excellent eyes to detail on this guide and editorial expertise are a blessing. Thank you.

To our writers groups, Parenting Awesome Kids group, and others who have brainstormed with us and shared ideas. Thank you.

Jonathan Bishop. Thank you for using your creativity to birth our emoji personality people.

Thank you, Gerry Wakeland and the CLASS family. Because of you, we have an understanding of the personalities that has allowed us to build and grow relationships in a deeper way.

A special thanks in remembrance of Florence Littauer, our mentor, encourager, and friend.

Recommended Resources

DeArmond, Deb and Ron. *Don't Go to Bed Angry.* Abingdon Press. 2016.

Farrel, Pam and Bill. *Marriage Meetups.* His and Her Set. Love-Wise Publishing, 2020.

Farrel, Pam. *Men Are Like Waffles--Women Are Like Spaghetti: Understanding and Delighting in Your Differences.* 2017.

Farrel, Pam. *52 Ways to Wow Your Husband: How to Put a Smile on His Face.* Harvest House. 2011.

Farrel, Pam. *Red-Hot Monogamy.* Harvest House. 2006.

Gilden, Linda and Goldfarb, Linda. *LINKED for Parents Quick Guide to Personalities: Maximizing Family Connections One Link at a Time.* Bold Vision Books. 2019.

Gilden, Linda. *Love Notes on His Pillow.* Rosebud Publishing. 2020.

Pritchard, Ray. *The Healing Power of Forgiveness: Let Go of Your Hurt Experience Renewed Relationships Find New Intimacy with God.* Harvest House Publishers. 2005.

Smalley, Gary. *Love as a Way of Life: Seven Keys to Transforming Every Aspect of Your Life.* Image Publishers. 2008.

Terkeurst, Lysa. *It's Not Supposed to Be This Way.* Thomas Nelson. 2018.

Thomas, Gary. *Sacred Marriage.* Zondervan. 2015.

Zook, Joyce. *12 Keys for Marriage Success, A Biblical Perspective for Wives.* 2019.

Other Resources

https://inspiration.org/christian-articles/5-cleaning-tips-to-spruce-up-your-relationship/

https://www.crosswalk.com/slideshows/our-top-10-mistakes-in-50-years-of-marriage-mckeever.html

Meet the Two Lindas of Personality

Linda Gilden

My introduction to the personalities over twenty years ago was life-changing. On discovering perfectionism was one of my Organizer traits, I realized that not only did I expect perfectionism of myself but of everyone around me. Once I understood my perfectionism, I was free to be me and let others do the same. I was able to be a better spouse as I allowed my husband to be who God intended him to be. I relaxed and focused on God's plan for my family rather than my perfection-driven plan. Marriage is an amazing gift from God, especially when you have the tools you need to do it well. Set goals for your marriage. Just remember not to set them too high or demand they be met every time. No marriage is perfect. But with God's guidance, a lot of effort and love, and understanding of who you and your spouse are, it will be a great marriage and perfect for you. Enjoy the ride!

Married mother of three adult children, "Rose" to the cutest grandchildren ever, Award-Winning Author, Speaker, Editor, Writing Coach, Writers

Conference Director, Certified Advanced Personalities Trainer and Consultant, Certified Writing Coach.

Linda Goldfarb

Studying and teaching the personalities for more than eighteen years has grown me relationally, professionally, and spiritually as a powerful Mobilizer. I've embraced listening more and talking less, and by doing so, I invite others to speak out with confidence. As a board-certified Christian life coach, I guide parents and professional clients, specific to their personalities, resulting in higher goals reached in a shorter timeframe. Communicating with my husband, children, and grandchildren is the best it's ever been. Now, it's your turn. I hope you're ready to connect with others in ways you've never done before!

Married mother of four adult children, "Maw-Maw" to many grandchildren, Award-Winning Author, International Speaker, Founder and Instructor of Parenting Awesome Kids, Board Certified Advanced Life Coach, Certified Advanced Personalities Trainer and Consultant.

More LINKED® PERSONALITY RESOURCES FOR YOU

VISIT LINKEDPERSONALITIES.COM.

Watch for more LINKED® Quick Guides coming soon.

LINKED® for Leaders Quick Guide
Maximizing Relational Skills One Link at a Time

LINKED® for Writers and Speakers Quick Guide
Maximizing Your Publishing and Presentation Skills

LINKED® for Teens Quick Guide
Maximizing Relationships One Link at a Time